Scientific Philosophy: A Theory Of Human Knowledge

Francis Ellingwood Abbot

In the interest of creating a more extensive selection of rare historical book reprints, we have chosen to reproduce this title even though it may possibly have occasional imperfections such as missing and blurred pages, missing text, poor pictures, markings, dark backgrounds and other reproduction issues beyond our control. Because this work is culturally important, we have made it available as a part of our commitment to protecting, preserving and promoting the world's literature. Thank you for your understanding.

SCIENTIFIC PHILOSOPHY:

A

Theory of Human Knowledge.

BY

FRANCIS ELLINGWOOD ABBOT, M.A., Ph.D.

REPRINTED FROM THE LONDON MIND
FOR OCTOBER, 1882.

SCIENTIFIC PHILOSOPHY:

A THEORY OF HUMAN KNOWLEDGE.

[*Reprinted from* MIND, *a Quarterly Journal of Psychology and Philosophy, No. XXVIII.*]

I.

IN the Preface to the Second Edition of the *Critique of Pure Reason*, Kant has this remarkable passage:—

"It has hitherto been assumed that our cognition must conform to the objects; but all attempts to ascertain anything about these *à priori*, by means of conceptions, and thus to extend the range of our knowledge, have been rendered abortive by this assumption. Let us then make the experiment whether we may not be more successful in metaphysics, if we assume that the objects must conform to our cognition. . . . We here propose to do just what Copernicus did in attempting to explain the celestial movements. When he found that he could make no progress by assuming that all the heavenly bodies revolved around the spectator, he reversed the process, and tried the experiment of assuming that the spectator revolved, while the stars remained at rest. We may make the same experiment with regard to the intuition of objects. If the intuition must conform to the nature of the objects, I do not see how we can know anything of them *à priori*. If, on the other hand, the object conforms to the nature of our faculty of intuition, I can then easily conceive the possibility of such an *à priori* knowledge. . . . This attempt to introduce a complete revolution in the procedure of metaphysics, after the example of the geometricians and natural philosophers, constitutes the aim of the Critique of Pure Speculative Reason."

Lange, in his *History of Materialism* (II. 156), thus alludes to the foregoing passage, and correctly states the conclusions logically deducible from it :

"Kant himself was very far from comparing himself with Kepler; but he made another comparison that is more significant and appropriate. He compared his achievement with that of Copernicus. But this achievement consisted in this, that he reversed the previous standpoint of metaphysics. Copernicus dared, 'by a paradoxical but yet true method,' to seek the observed motions, not in the heavenly bodies, but in their observers. Not less 'paradoxical' must it appear to the sluggish mind of man, when Kant lightly and certainly *overturns our collective experience, with all the historical and exact sciences* [the italics are ours], by the simple assumption that our notions do not regulate themselves according to things, but things according to our notions. It follows immediately from this that the objects of experience altogether are only *our* objects; that the whole objective world is, in a word, not absolute objectivity, but only objectivity for man and any similarly organised beings, while, behind the phenomenal world, the absolute nature of things, the 'thing-in-itself,' is veiled in impenetrable darkness."

Now when the great Kant, whose towering and consummate genius there is no one to dispute, founded the Critical Philosophy on this cardinal doctrine that "things conform to cognition, not cognition to things," and when he claimed thereby to have created a mighty "revolution" in philosophy comparable only with that of Copernicus in astronomy, did he really occupy a new philosophical standpoint, or really adopt a new philosophical method?

No. On the contrary, he merely completed, organised, and formulated the veritable revolution which was initiated in the latter half of the eleventh century by Roscellinus the Nominalist, —which was condemned in his person by the Realist Council of Soissons, revived in the fourteenth century by William of Occam, and finally made triumphant in philosophy towards the end of the fifteenth century, not so much by the inherent strength of Nominalism as by the weakness of its expiring rival, Scholastic Realism.

The essence of Nominalism was the doctrine that universals, or terms denoting genera and species, correspond to nothing really existent outside of the mind, but are either mere empty names (Extreme Nominalism) or names denoting mere subjective concepts (Moderate Nominalism or Conceptualism). Nominalism distinctly anticipated the Critical Philosophy in referring the source of all general conceptions (and thereby of all human knowledge), not to the object alone or to the object and subject together, but to the subject alone; it distinctly anticipated the doctrine that "things conform to cognition, not cognition to things". Since genera and species are classifications of things based on their supposed resemblances and differences, the denial of all objective reality to genera and species is the denial of all objective reality to the supposed resemblances and differences of things themselves; the denial of all knowledge of the relations of objects is the denial of all knowledge of the objects related; and this denial is tantamount to the assertion that things-in-themselves are utterly unknown.

Wrapped up in the essential doctrine of Nominalism, therefore, was the doctrine that things-in-themselves are utterly unknown; that the knowledge of their supposed resemblances and differences is derived only from the supposing mind; that "things conform to cognition, not cognition to things"; in short, that the only knowledge possible to man is the knowledge of the à priori constitution of his own mind, and the relations which it imposes upon things (if they exist), totally irrespective of what things really are.

Nothing can be plainer, then, than that the Critical Philosophy did but logically develop the prime tenet of Nominalism, formulate it successfully, and expand it to a self-consistent philosophical system. This, and this alone, was the true merit of Kant. The "revolution" by which philosophy was made to transfer its fundamental standpoint from the world of things to the world of thought, and in consequence of which modern philosophy in both its great schools has inherited an irresistible tendency towards Idealism, had been substantially effected and definitely established some four hundred years before. Kant did but bring to flower and fruitage the seed sown by Roscellinus, and his Critical Philosophy was only the logical evolution and outcome of Mediæval Nominalism.

By Kant's masterly development of Nominalism into a great philosophical system, it has exercised upon subsequent speculation a constantly increasing power. In truth, all modern philosophy, by tacit agreement, rests upon the Nominalistic theory of universals. Hence alone can be explained the fact, so patent and so striking, yet so little understood or even inquired into, that both the great schools of modern philosophy, the Transcendental and the Associational, equally exhibit in its full force the tendency to Idealism latent in that theory. Nominalism logically reduces all experience, actual or possible, to a mere subjective affection of the individual Ego, and does not permit even the Ego to know itself as a noumenon. The historical development of the Critical Philosophy into the subjective idealism of Fichte, the objective idealism of Schelling, and the absolute idealism of Hegel, only shows how impossible it is for that philosophy to overstep the magic circle of Egoism with which Nominalism logically environed itself. No less striking is the inability of the English school to escape from the idealistic tendencies inherent in its purely subjective principle of Association—one of the innumerable *aliases* by which Nominalism eludes detection at the bar of contemporary thought; for Locke's successors, Berkeley, Hume, Hartley, the Mills, Bain, Spencer, and others, drift towards Idealism as steadily as Kant and his successors. It is, in fact, logically impossible to draw any but idealistic conclusions from the premisses of Nominalism—and those, too, idealistic conclusions which can not stop short of absolute Solipsism.

That modern philosophy in both its great branches irresistibly tends to Idealism is a position that will scarcely be disputed. Dr. Krauth, in his admirable edition of Berkeley's *Principles of Human Knowledge* (p. 122), thus sums up the grounds of this general and admitted tendency, while yet not perceiving that in the last analysis they are all reducible to the almost universal acceptance of the Nominalistic view of genera and species, with its implied negation of the objectivity of relations :—

"It (Idealism) rests on *generally* recognised principles in regard to consciousness. Its definition of consciousness is the one most widely received: the mind's recognition of its own conditions. It maintains that the cognitions of consciousness are absolute and infallible, and that nothing but these is, in their *degree*, knowledge. In all these postulates the great mass of thinkers agree with Idealism. The foundation of Idealism is the common foundation of nearly all the developed philosophical thinking of all schools. Idealism declares that, while consciousness is infallible, our interpretations of it, on which we base *inferences*, may be incorrect; and nearly all thinkers of all schools agree with Idealism here. No inference, or class of inferences, in which a mistake ever occurs is a basis of positive knowledge. Hence, says Idealism, only that which is directly in consciousness is positively known, and nothing is directly in consciousness but the mind's own states. Therefore we *know* nothing more. So completely has this general conviction taken possession of the philosophical mind, that even antagonists of Idealism, who would cut *it* up by the roots if they could cut *this* up, have not pretended that it could be done." (The italics are all Dr. Krauth's.)

The "strength of Idealism," thus described by Dr. Krauth, is the strength of Nominalism—no more, no less. If all the general and special relations of things, conceived by the mind and expressed by general terms, exist in the mind alone, nothing is known of things themselves; for knowledge of things is knowledge of their relations. Nominalism, therefore, is the original source of the definition of knowledge adopted by Idealism, as shown above: that is, the contents of consciousness alone. Inasmuch, moreover, as the notion of a *common* consciousness is itself a general notion, and consequently destitute of all objectivity, nothing is "knowledge," so defined, that is outside of the *individual* consciousness. Beginning with Nominalism, therefore, Idealism must end in Solipsism, on penalty of stultifying itself by arbitrary self-contradiction. This was the path marked out for the Critical Philosophy by inexorable logic, and Fichte was more Kantian than Kant himself when he resolutely pursued it. Solipsism is the very *reductio ad absurdum* of Idealism, yet it is the rigorously logical consequence of its own definition of knowledge, which again is the rigorously logical consequence of the Nominalistic view of universals. On this point, a further quotation from Dr. Krauth will be extremely pertinent :—

"While Idealism has here a speculative strength, which it is not wise to ignore, it is not without its weakness, even at this very point, for its history shows that it is rarely willing to stand unreservedly by the results of its own principle as regards consciousness. If it accept only the direct and infallible knowledge supplied in consciousness, it has no common ground left but this—that there is the one train of ideas, which passes in the consciousness of a particular individual. A consistent Idealist can claim to know no more than this—that there exist ideas in his consciousness. He cannot know that he has a substantial personal existence, or that there is any other being, finite or infinite, beside himself. And as many Idealists are not satisfied with maintaining that we do not know that there is an external world, but go further, and declare that we know that there is not an external world, they must for consistency's sake hold that an Idealist knows that there is nothing, thing or person, beside himself. Solipsism, or absolute Egoism, with the exclusion of proper personality, is the logic of Idealism, if the inferential be excluded. But if *inference*, in any degree whatever, be allowed, not only would the natural logic and natural inference of most men sweep away Idealism, but its own principle of knowledge is subverted by the terms of the supposition. Idealism stands or falls by the principle that *no inference is knowledge*. We may reach inferences by knowledge, but we can never reach knowledge by inference" (p. 123).

Against both schools of modern philosophy, therefore, committed as they both are to the definition of knowledge drawn from Nominalism and ending in Solipsism, the charge of logical inconsistency and self-contradiction may be fairly brought, just so far as they hesitate to follow up the path to cloudland which begins with that definition. But any philosophy which hesitates to be logical forfeits all claim to the respectful consideration of mankind.

The great Roscellino-Kantian "revolution" by which Nominalism was made to supplant Scholastic Realism, and philosophy to transfer its fundamental standpoint from the world of things to the world of thought, was a revolution which logically contracts "human knowledge" to the petty dimensions of individual self-consciousness—renders it valueless as to things themselves and valuable only as to the *à priori* constitution of the individual's own mind—and in effect reduces it to a grand hallucination. Like the French Revolution, the Nominalistic revolution can live only by the guillotine, and decapitates every perception which pretends to bring to the miserable solipsist, shut up in the prison of his own consciousness, the slightest information as to the great outside world. Defining knowledge as the mere contents of consciousness, it relegates to non-entity, as pseudo-knowledge, whatever claims to be more than that. Under its sway, philosophy is blind to the race, and beholds the individual alone. What wonder that, in the hands of those who insist on their rights to reduce theory to practice, philosophy is so often found pandering to the moral lawlessness of an Individualism that sets mere personal opinion above the supreme ethical sanctities of the universe? In human society, individual autonomy is universal antinomy; for the law that binds only one binds none. Yet, with Nominalism for its root, Idealism for its flower, and Solipsism for its fruit, how can modern philosophy, teaching in both its great schools that the individual mind knows nothing except the states of its own consciousness, discover any law that shall have recognised authority over all consciousness? For such a discovery it is hopelessly incompetent. So far, therefore, as the social and moral interests of mankind are concerned, the present philosophical situation has become simply intolerable.

Fortunately for the future of society, however, the principle of cognition embodied in the Nominalistic definition of knowledge has never obtained general assent outside of the circle of purely speculative thought. The protest of "common sense" against it was even taken up by the Scotch school in the name of philosophy itself; but the same Nominalism which paralyses all modern philosophy paralysed the Scotch school, and the protest died on its tongue. Without any conscious protest, however, though with an instinctive hostility to "metaphysics" and to the philosophy which it confounds with "metaphysics," physical science has immovably planted itself on a new definition of knowledge, and fortified it impregnably against all comers; and, on the principle of cognition which it establishes, universal science, carrying up the physical and the mental into the higher unity of the cosmical, is even now beginning to build a temple of truth destined to be coæval with the human race.

(1) Modern Philosophy defines knowledge as the recognition by the Ego of its own conscious states.

(2) Modern science defines knowledge as twofold,—*individual knowledge*, or the mind's cognition of its own conscious states plus its cognition of the Cosmos of which it is a part, and *universal knowledge*, or the sum of all human cognitions of the Cosmos which have been substantiated by verification and certified by the unanimous consensus of the competent.

(This latter definition may never have been formulated before, but it is tacitly assumed in all investigations conducted according to the scientific method; and the results of that method would be completely invalidated, if the definition itself should be essentially erroneous. Science does not present its truths as anybody's "states of consciousness," but as cosmical facts, acknowledgment of which is binding upon all sane minds. The principle of cognition on which it proceeds is utterly antagonistic to the Nominalism which denies all objectivity to genera and species: it is drawn from Realism alone, not the Scholastic Realism of the Middle Ages, but the Scientific Realism or Relationism which will be explained below. Nominalism teaches that things conform to cognition, not cognition to things; Scientific Realism teaches that cognition conforms to things, not things to cognition. It is futile to seek a reconciliation of these positions; the contradiction is absolute and insoluble. " Modern philosophy counts nothing as "known" which is outside of the individual consciousness; modern science presents as "known" a vast mass of truths, of which only an insignificant fraction can be to-day comprised within the narrow limits of a single consciousness, and which in their totality can be contained only in the universal mind of man. Under the influence of the all-prevailing Nominalism of the present day, philosophy has, and must have, its beginning-point in the individual Ego; under the influence of its own unsuspected Realism, science begins with a Cosmos of which the individual Ego is merely a part. The one is exclusively and narrowly subjective, just so far as it is logically faithful to its own clearly proclaimed principle of cognition; the other is objective, in a sense so broad as to include the subjective within itself. In truth, so far was the old battle of Nominalism and Realism from being fought out by the end of the fifteenth century, that it is to-day the deep, underlying problem of problems, on the right solution of which depends the life of philosophy itself in the ages to come. But let it not be forgotten that the old Realism of Scholasticism is by no means the new Realism of science; the former perished as rightfully before Nominalism as Nominalism itself will perish before the latter.

That the scientific point of view is a thoroughly objective one, and that the cosmical facts discovered by science can by no means be made to vanish in the universal solvent of Nominalistic subjectivism, easily appears. One or two illustrations will suffice.

Prof. Jevons, in the *Principles of Science* (3rd ed., pp. 8, 9), thus speaks of the objective validity of mathematical formulae:—

"A mathematician certainly does treat of symbols, but only as the instruments whereby to facilitate his reasoning concerning quantities ; and as the axioms and rules of mathematical science must be verified in concrete objects in order that the calculations founded upon them may have any validity or utility, it follows that the ultimate objects of mathematical science are the things themselves. . . . Signs, thoughts, and exterior objects may be regarded as parallel and analogous series of phenomena, and to treat any one of the three series is equivalent to treating either of the other series."

Prof. Tyndall, in his *Light and Electricity* (pp. 60, 61), thus illustrates the unhesitating and unconditional objectivity with which the science of physics presents its truths, as facts of a veritably existent and actually known Cosmos :—

"The justification of a theory consists in its exclusive competence to account for phenomena. On such a basis the Wave Theory, or the Undulatory Theory of Light, now rests, and every day's experience only makes its foundations more secure. . . . This substance is called the luminiferous ether. It fills space ; it surrounds the atoms of bodies ; it extends, without solution of continuity, through the humors of the eye. The molecules of luminous bodies are in a state of vibration. The vibrations are taken up by the ether, and transmitted through it in waves. These waves impinging on the retina excite the sensation."

Prof. Cooke, in his *New Chemistry*, illustrates the same point still more strikingly and emphatically, with reference to the atomic theory :—

"The new chemistry assumes as its fundamental postulate that the magnitudes we call molecules are realities, but this is the only postulate. Grant the postulate, and you will find that all the rest follows as a necessary deduction. Deny it, and the 'New Chemistry' can have no meaning for you, and it is not worth your while to pursue the subject further. If, therefore, we would become imbued with the spirit of the new philosophy of chemistry, we must begin by believing in molecules ; and, if I have succeeded in setting forth in a clear light the fundamental truth that the molecules of chemistry are definite masses of matter, whose weight can be accurately determined, our time has been well spent."

Remembering that the weight of the hydrogen-atom is taken as the unit of molecular weight, or microcrith, and that, according to calculations based on the figures of Sir William Thomson, this atom weighs approximately, in decimals of a gramme, 0·000,000,000,000,000,000,000,109,312, or 109,312 octillionths of a gramme, one can easily perceive the impossibility of construing this utterly unimaginable quantity under any terms expressive of human consciousness. To consciousness it is equivalent to absolute zero; but the 'New Chemistry' demands belief in it as an actual quantity in Nature, an objectively existent reality in a Cosmos not resolvable into consciousness by any Nominalistic legerdemain.

It would be superfluous to cite further passages in order to illustrate the thoroughly objective spirit, method, and results of modern science, as contrasted with those of modern philosophy. All scientific investigations are founded on a theory diametrically opposed to that of Kant: namely, that things can be known, though incompletely known, as they are in themselves, and that cognition must conform itself to them, not they to it. This is the philosophical translation of the principle of verification. The Nominalism that inculcates the contrary doctrine is an excrescence upon modern philosophy, a cancerous tumour feeding upon its life. Science has achieved all its marvellous triumphs by practically denying the fundamental principle laid down by Kant, and by practically proceeding upon its exact opposite; and it is a scandal to philosophy that she has not yet legitimated this practical procedure, overwhelmingly justified as it is by its incontrovertible results. The time has come for philosophy to reverse the Roscellino-Kantian revolution, and give to science a theory of knowledge which shall render the scientific method, not practically successful (for that it already is), but theoretically impregnable. The present article is the beginning of an attempt in that direction. A glance at the course of speculation in the past will render clearer the nature of the problem which philosophy has now to solve.

II.

The pre-Socratic philosophy of Greece was unqualified Realism, of a *naïve* and primitive type. The earlier Ionic philosophers, Thales, Anaximander, and Anaximenes, sought only to generalise the phenomena of the outer world, as products of a single original cause or principle ($\dot{\alpha}\rho\chi\acute{\eta}$)—water, undifferentiated chaotic matter ($\tau\grave{o}$ $\ddot{\alpha}\pi\epsilon\iota\rho o\nu$), air,—but they never dreamed of doubting its objective existence. The Pythagoreans sought the causal unity of the universe in its most general relations, as number, proportion, harmony, order, law, which they conceived as at once the abstract and concrete directive force of nature; their cosmology was no less objective than that of their predecessors. The Eleatics, Xenophanes, Parmenides, Zeno of Elea, Melissus, maintained the principle of objective Monism; their $\overset{"}{\epsilon}\nu$ $\kappa\alpha\grave{\iota}$ $\pi\hat{\alpha}\nu$ was illimitable and immutable Being, devoid of every positive attribute save that of thought, while the manifold appearances under which it presents itself to man were only mere seeming and delusion. But there was no element of subjectivism in their cosmology; they attributed to the cosmos permanence without change, unity without multiplicity, as its constitutive objective principle. Heraclitus taught that the principle of all things was fire, as the type of ceaseless and universal change ($\pi\acute{\alpha}\nu\tau\alpha$ $\chi\omega\rho\epsilon\hat{\iota}$), in opposition to the Eleatics; but his cosmology was none the less objective because he discovered in it only change without permanence, multiplicity without unity. Empedocles sought to mediate between the Eleatic and Heraclitean views by positing four changeless elements, air, earth, fire and water, with two constant forces, love and hate, and by conceding endless change in the combinations and mutual relations of these permanent factors of creation; but he was wholly as realistic and objective as his predecessors. The Atomists, Leucippus and Democritus, offered a strictly mechanical explanation of Nature, attributing independent objective reality to the atoms which alone remained changeless in the midst of eternal change. Anaxagoras in a certain sense summed up all the preceding philosophies in his own, by means of his theory of ὁμοιομέρειαι or *semina rerum*, while he introduced a new principle in the assumption of an immaterial νοῦς as the moving and guiding cause of the universe; and he, too, was unreservedly objective in his cosmology.

With the Sophists, however, appeared the first symptoms of true subjectivism; and they may be regarded as the forerunners of Nominalism, though only in a feeble, crude, and undeveloped sense. The Sophists had no system, no school, no determinate principle save that of scepticism as to objective truth and paradoxical acquiescence in all opinions as equally true or equally false. Their movement was the destructive distillation of all fixed conviction in the heats of logomachy and interminable word-quibbling. They had nothing in common save a certain unity of spirit and method—a spirit of universal scepticism, and a method of adroit disputation by the employment of double meanings and ambiguous middle terms. Sceptics in philosophy, anarchists in ethics, their greatest historical merit is that of having polarised and called into activity the noble intellect of Socrates. They held no definite theory of subjectivism at all; but the manner in which they evacuated *general terms* of all fixed meaning and all objective validity challenged and arrested the attention of Socrates, as the true secret of their plausibility and bewildering success in debate. It was this fact that fixed and determined the direction taken by this mighty genius. The Sophists practically, though not theoretically, anticipated the Nominalists in conceding only subjective validity to generic and specific terms, which constitute the very alphabet of knowledge; and Socrates, piercing to the ulterior consequences of this procedure in the dissolution of all intellectual verity and all moral obligation, rose, like a giant in his strength, to combat a great tendency of his time which threatened to cause the fatty degeneration of Greek civilisation, the melancholy decay of Greek thought and life.

The astounding success of Socrates in this great struggle is the most splendid monument to the power of individual genius that the history of philosophy can show. Alone and unaided, he checked and reversed the Nominalistic revolution already far advanced, annihilated the Sophists as a practical power in philosophy, and determined the course of speculation for a millennium and a half in the direction of Realism. No other victory such as this was ever won in the annals of human thought; and yet what historian of philosophy has perceived, much less celebrated it? It will never be appreciated until the dominant Nominalism of modern philosophy has given place to the dawning New Realism of modern science—a day perhaps less distant than now appears. What gave success to Socrates in this vast encounter was the fact that he planted himself on an immovable rock, the objective significance and validity of general terms, as opposed to their purely subjective import and value. Even Schwegler, blind as he is to the enormous importance of the struggle between Nominalism and Realism (to which in his *History of Philosophy* he devotes less than one page!), says of Socrates that "there begins with him the *philosophy of objective thought*" (p. 38, Stirling's Translation—the italics are his). Aristotle explicitly declares in the *Metaphysics* (XII. 4) that "Socrates was engaged in forming systems in regard to the ethical or moral virtues, and was the first to institute an investigation in regard to the universal definition of these. . . . There are two improvements in science which one might justly ascribe to Socrates—I allude to his employment of inductive arguments and his definition of the universal. . . . Socrates did not, it is true, constitute universals a thing involving a separate subsistence, nor did he regard the definitions as such; the other philosophers, however, invested them with a separate subsistence." But Socrates did attribute universal objective authority to the virtues he defined; he refuted the Sophistic construction of them as merely subjective; he repudiated the Sophistic notion that nothing is good or bad by nature ($\phi\acute{v}\sigma\epsilon\iota$), but only by statute ($\nu\acute{o}\mu\varphi$), and vindicated the objectivity of general terms *in some sense*, without reaching that luminous doctrine of the objectivity of relations which alone explains it clearly. That Socrates conceived of universals as objective realities, without arriving at any definite concluions as to the mode of this reality, sufficiently appears from the subsequent course of Plato and Aristotle, both of whom inherited from Socrates the undefined objectivity of universals, and each of whom proceeded to define it in his own way. The point to be here specially noted is the fact that Socrates rolled back the advancing tide of Nominalism let loose by the Sophists, accomplished the feat by means of the definition of universals as objectively valid and real, and stamped the thought of fifteen hundred years with the impress of his own Realism.

The impending Nominalistic revolution having been thus definitely arrested by Socrates,—the great question of universals having been bequeathed by him to succeeding generations for a full and final solution,—the existence of an objective outer world was a common and undisputed premiss among his followers. In particular, the assumption of the objective reality of genera and species, as necessarily involved in that of a cognisable outer world, and as constituting the objective ground of all general terms, became a common point of departure to Plato and Aristotle. But, while Plato erected on this assumption his theory of Ideas, Aristotle erected on it his opposing theory of Essences or Forms—to which reference will be more particularly made below. Both the Platonic and Aristotelian points of view were fundamentally and equally objective, and equally alien to the point occupied by modern philosophy since the triumph of Nominalism over Realism, when the tides of thought began to set irresistibly in the direction of subjectivism.

The Stoics betrayed to some extent the influence of the Sophists in their theory of universals. They discarded alike the Platonic theory of Ideas and the Aristotelian theory of Forms, and were apparently the first to proclaim distinctly the doctrine of subjective concepts, formed through abstraction. This doctrine, however, did not attain in their hands a full logical development into the theory of Nominalism; in fact, it did not at all prevent the Stoics from advancing to the construction of a positively objective cosmology and theology of their own; and, although with a serious logical inconsistency, they maintained on the whole an objective point of view.

The Epicureans, with their doctrine of the atoms and the truth of all perceptions of matter, may be considered quite free from the tendency to subjectivism, so far as the present discussion is concerned.

The Sceptics—the earlier with their "Ten Tropes," and the later with their "Five Tropes"—did not so much deny the existence of an outer world as the trustworthiness of human knowledge of it, and advanced no definite doctrine respecting universals. They occupied mainly negative and critical ground, and exerted no great influence in that controversy. Their arguments mostly rest on the assumption of Realism.

During the third great period of Greek philosophy, including the Græco-Judaic, the Neo-Pythagorean, and the Neo-Platonic schools, the predominant tendency was pre-eminently objective, since the mystical or theosophical contemplation of a Divine

Transcendent Object by means of the "ecstatic intuition" is incompatible with an exclusive subjectivity. (Theosophy, in fact, tends to reduce the subject to a state of pure passivity,) and to absorb him completely in contemplation of the Object of worship.

In no period of Greek philosophy, therefore, did the Nominalistic tendency gain much force or headway after it had once been checked by Socrates. Its hour had not yet come.

Passing now to the Christian Era, it may be said that the Patristic period was devoted to the development of systematic or dogmatic theology, without interference from pagan philosophy after the closing of the School at Athens, in A.D. 529, by edict of the emperor Justinian. Since dogmatic theology, by the very nature of its conceptions, is unqualifiedly objective, the Patristic and in main the Scholastic periods are chiefly noticeable here as having carried the principle of objectivity to so abnormal and oppressive a degree of development as to cause speculation to rebound to the opposite extreme. The creation of a great body of doctrine held by the Catholic Church to be the absolute and unmixed truth of God, and the terrible intolerance with which the Church stamped out all dissent from this fixed standard of belief, inevitably tended to excite a reaction against it, in proportion to the mental activity of the age. Moreover, the Church had planted itself in philosophy upon the Realism of Plato and Aristotle; and it was equally inevitable that the reaction should be against this, no less than against the theology of the Church. There is no room for wonder, then, at the fact that the cause of Nominalism came to be identified with the cause of intellectual and religious freedom, and the triumph of the one with the triumph of the other. Consequently it is to the Scholastic period, and to the rise of the great controversy between Realism and Nominalism—the former representing Catholic orthodoxy and the latter heterodoxy,—that must be traced the beginning of the general subjective movement of modern philosophy, although this movement did not gain full headway till after the downfall of Scholasticism, when victorious Nominalism had time to develop unrestrained all the latent tendencies it involved. Tennemann has significantly and truly said that this momentous controversy was "never definitely settled". The reason is that both sides were right, yet neither wholly so; they did but bequeath to later times a problem they could not solve. Disguised as it is by new forms and new names, the immeasurably important issue between objectivism and subjectivism involved in that ancient controversy survives to-day. Nominalism, by virtue of the truth it contained and the freedom it represented, conquered Realism in philosophy, and culminated in the splendid genius of Kant; Realism, by virtue of the truth it too contained, conquered Nominalism in science, created an army of experimental investigators of Nature, and culminated in the establishment of the scientific method, which, though as yet purely practical and empirical, demands with increasing emphasis from philosophy a theory of knowledge that shall justify it in all eyes. Here is the explanation of the wide divergence, the virtual divorce and even antagonism, which is so patent a fact to all who look beneath the surface of things, between science and philosophy. All the intellectual interests of mankind must suffer greatly, until the breach is effectually healed; and the first step to the reconciliation so much to be desired must be a clear comprehension of the causes which have created the division. Hence the necessity of surveying the ancient battle-field of Scholasticism.

The proximate origin of the great mediæval dispute over the nature of universals seems to have been a passage at the commencement of Porphyry's *Introduction* to Aristotle's treatise on the *Categories*, known at the time only through the Latin translation of Boëthius, in which these three problems were stated, but not elucidated, with respect to genera and species:—
" (1) Whether they have a substantive existence, or reside merely in naked mental conceptions. (2) Whether, assuming them to have substantive existence, they are bodies or incorporeals. (3) Whether their substantive existence is in and along with the objects of sense, or apart and separable." Neglecting minor distinctions, refinements and subtleties, and without following the long and tedious course of the dispute, it will amply suffice for present purposes to state concisely the five leading positions maintained by different philosophers of the Scholastic period, as follows :—

(1) EXTREME REALISM *(Universalia ante rem)* taught that universals were substances or things, existing independently of and separable from particulars or individuals. This was the essence of Plato's Theory of Ideas, and Plato was the father of Extreme Realism as held in the Scholastic period. Scotus Erigena, who died A.D. 880, was the first to revive this doctrine in the Schools, borrowing from the Pseudo-Dionysius Areopagita.

(2) MODERATE REALISM *(Universalia in re)* also taught that universals were substances, but only as dependent upon and inseparable from individuals, in which each inhered; that is, each universal inhered in each of the particulars ranged under it. This was the theory of Aristotle, who held that the τόδε τι

or individual thing was the First Essence, while universals were only Second Essences, real in a less complete sense than First Essences. He thus reversed the Platonic doctrine, which attributed the fullest reality to universals only, and a merely "participative" reality to individuals. Until Scotus Erigena resuscitated the Platonic theory, Aristotle's was the received doctrine in the Schools; and the warfare was simply between those two forms of Realism prior to the advent of Roscellinus.

(3) EXTREME NOMINALISM *(Universalia post rem)* taught that universals had no substantive or objective existence at all, but were merely empty names or words *(nomina, voces, flatus vocis)*. Though probably not the absolute originator of this *sententia vocum*, as the doctrine came to be called, Roscellinus, Canon of Compiègne, was the first to give it currency and notoriety, and the Council of Soissons, under the influence of the Realist Anselm of Canterbury, his chief opponent, forced him in the year 1092 to recant the tritheistic interpretation of the Trinity, which he had consistently and courageously avowed. The theory of Extreme Nominalism was thus put under the ecclesiastical ban.

(4) MODERATE NOMINALISM or CONCEPTUALISM *(Universalia post rem)* taught that universals have no substantive existence at all, but yet are more than mere names signifying nothing; and that they exist really, though only subjectively, as concepts in the mind, of which names are the vocal symbols. Abélard is claimed by some, but probably incorrectly, as the author of this modification of the Nominalistic view; William of Occam, who died in 1347, seems to have been the chief, if not the earliest, representative of it. The *Encyclopædia Britannica* (xvi., 284, 8th ed.) says: "The theory termed Conceptualism, or conceptual Nominalism, was really the one maintained by all succeeding Nominalists, and is the doctrine of ideas generally believed in at the present day".

(5) Albertus Magnus (died 1280), Thomas Aquinas (died 1274), Duns Scotus (died 1308), and others fused all these views into one, and taught that universals exist in a three-fold manner: *Universalia ante rem*, as thoughts in the mind of God; *Universalia in re*, as the essence (quiddity) of things, according to Aristotle; and *Universalia post rem*, as concepts in the sense of Moderate Nominalism. This is to-day the orthodox philosophy of the Catholic Church, as opposed to the prevailingly exclusive Conceptualism of the Protestant world.

Thus both Extreme Realism and Moderate Realism maintained the objective reality of genera and species; while both Extreme Nominalism and Moderate Nominalism maintained that genera and species possess no objective reality at all.

In contrast with all the views above presented, another and sixth view will now be stated, which, taken as a whole and with reference to the vitally important consequences it involves, is believed to be both novel and true.

(6) RELATIONISM or SCIENTIFIC REALISM (of which *universalia inter res* may be adopted as an apt formula) teaches that universals, or genera and species, are, *first*, objective relations of resemblance among objectively existing things; *secondly*, subjective concepts of these relations, determined in the mind by the relations themselves; and, *thirdly*, names representative both of the relations and the concepts, and applicable alike to both. This is the view logically implied in all scientific classifications of natural objects, regarded as objects of real scientific knowledge. But although empirically employed with dazzling success in the investigation of Nature, it does not appear to have been ever theoretically generalised or stated.

This view rests for its justification upon a broader principle; namely, that of the *Objectivity of Relations*, as opposed to the principle of the *Subjectivity of Relations*, which is the essence of the Nominalistic doctrine of universals inculcated by modern philosophy. Kant distinctly made "Relation" one of the four forms of the logical judgment which determine the twelve "categories of the understanding"; *i.e.*, the *à priori* forms of thought, totally independent of "things-in-themselves," and applicable to them only so far as they are objects of a possible "experience," which, however, reveals nothing of their real nature. This doctrine that relations do not inhere at all in "things-in-themselves," but are simply imposed upon them by the mind in experience as the purely subjective form of phenomena, is strictly deducible from the Nominalistic doctrine that general terms, by which relations are expressed, correspond to nothing objectively real; and Kant's master-mind is nowhere more clearly apparent than in the subtlety and profundity with which he thus seized the prevalent but undeveloped Nominalism of the modern period, and erected it into the most imposing philosophical system of the world. By this doctrine of the Subjectivity of Relations, Kant reduced the outer world to utterly unknown *Dinge-an-sich*, and paved the way for his still more thorough-going disciple, Fichte, to deny their very existence, and thereby to take a great stride in conducting Nominalism to its only logical terminus, Solipsism.

The principle of Relationism, however, rests on these self-evident propositions:—

(1) Relations are absolutely inseparable from their terms.
(2) The relations of things are absolutely inseparable from the things themselves.

[handwritten: # (6) There is, however, a Relation between things Existing Subjectively & things Existing Objectively.]

(3) The relations of things must exist where the things themselves are, whether objectively in the Cosmos or subjectively in the mind.
(4) If things exist objectively, their relations must exist objectively; but if their relations are merely subjective, the things themselves must be merely subjective.
(5) There is no logical alternative between affirming the objectivity of relations in and with that of things, and denying the objectivity of things in and with that of relations.

For instance, a triangle consists of six elements, three sides and three angles. The sides are things; the angles are relations —relations of greater or less divergence between the sides. If the sides exist objectively, the angles must exist objectively also; but if the angles are merely subjective, so must the sides be also. To affirm that the sides are objective realities, even as incognisable things-in-themselves, while yet the angles, as relations, have only a subjective existence, is the *ne plus ultra* of logical absurdity. Yet Kantianism, Nominalism, and all Nominalistic philosophy, are driven irresistibly to that very conclusion.

In short, it is because modern philosophy rests exclusively on the basis of Nominalism, of which the only logical terminus is absolute Egoistic Idealism or Solipsism, and because modern science rests exclusively on the basis of Relationism, that we affirm unqualifiedly an irreconcilable antagonism between the two just so long as their respective bases remain unchanged. It seems needless, but may be nevertheless advisable, to point out explicitly that Relationism carefully shuns the great error of Scholastic Realism, *i.e.*, the hypostasisation of universals as substances, entities, or things; it teaches that genera and species exist objectively, but only as relations, and that things and relations constitute two great, distinct orders of objective reality, inseparable in existence, yet distinguishable in thought.

The philosophic value of the principle of Relationism is strikingly illustrated in the ease with which, applied as a key, it unlocks the secret and lays bare the signification of the ancient and still unfinished controversy between Realism and Nominalism.
(1) It shows that Extreme Realism was right in upholding the objectivity of universals, but wrong in classing them as independent and separable substances or things.
(2) It shows that Moderate Realism was right in upholding the objectivity of universals, but wrong in making them inherent in individuals AS INDIVIDUALS *(in re)* rather

than in individuals AS GROUPS *(inter res)*. Relations do not inhere in either of the related terms taken singly, but do inhere in all the terms taken collectively.

(3) It shows that Extreme Nominalism was right in denying the objectivity of universals as substances or things (the great error of its opponent), and right in affirming the existence of universals as names; but wrong in denying their objectivity as relations and their subjectivity as concepts.

(4) It shows that Moderate Nominalism or Conceptualism was right in denying the objectivity of universals as substances, and also right in affirming their subjectivity as concepts; but wrong in denying their objectivity as relations.

Thus every element of truth is gathered up, and every element of error is eliminated, by rejecting the four historic theories already recapitulated, together with the merely syncretistic fifth theory, and by substituting in their place the propounded sixth theory of Relationism. Its precision, lucidity, comprehensiveness, and adequacy to account for all the facts, will become so evident to anyone patient enough to master it fully in all its bearings, as to warrant the indulgence of a hope that it may permanently solve the great problem declared by Tennemann to have never been "definitively settled".

III.

When Scholasticism fell, the theory of Relationism had occurred to no one. Each of the competing theories discerned the weakness of its rivals, yet could not discern its own, and was therefore unable to arrive at the real truth respecting universals. Consequently, as has just been pointed out, the truth was divided among them. Nominalism gradually won the ascendancy among philosophers in the form of Conceptualism; while Relationism became, not indeed a received theory, since as a theory it did not yet exist, but yet the unformulated and empirical principle of the actual practice of scientific observers, experimenters, and investigators of nature. Philosophy divorced itself from a true objectivity, and surrendered itself to subjectivism in the form of Moderate Nominalism; while science, ceasing to philosophise, turned its back upon the barren metaphysics of the schools, because they could yield no objective knowledge, and learned the sad lesson of contempt for philosophy itself.

A period of transition followed the downfall of Scholasticism, full of confusion and conflicting tendencies. Spasmodic resuscitation of various ancient philosophies—Aristotelianism in a more accurately known form, Platonism, Neo-Platonism, Stoicism, Epicureanism, &c.—ensued; but these revived systems did not materially contribute to the growth of the subjective tendency, since, as has been shown, ancient philosophy in the post-Socratic periods had been prevailingly objective in all its forms. The true origin of the increasing subjectivism of philosophy, and therefore the true secret of the increasing repugnance of science for philosophy itself, lay in the triumph of Nominalism over the relatively inferior Realism of the Middle Ages, in its denial of all objective knowledge save of particulars *as isolated and unrelated*, and in its claim of a strictly subjective genesis for universals as concepts or names alone. Philosophy in this manner stripped the objective world of everything that was really intelligible—genera, species, relations of all kinds; while science, bereft of all philosophical aid, took refuge in a rude sort of common sense and fortified itself in a spirit of defiance to all speculative thought. Bacon's popularity rested really on no stronger foundation: he merely headed an unreasoning revolt against Nominalism, hardly knowing what he did, yet practically rendering an immense service by rallying the enterprising and curious spirits of the time about the standard of "induction". He too joined in the wide-spread outcry against Aristotle and his followers, mistakenly believing that Aristotle was really responsible for the Nominalism of the age which he vaguely felt to be the chief obstacle to science. The results of this open feud between science and philosophy were disastrous to both in the end; for, while the latter tended steadily towards Idealism and Solipsism, the former as steadily tended towards Materialism. For the time being, however, the revolt of science against philosophy was most salutary.

While science adopted a purely empirical objective method, took Nature for granted, investigated things and their relations by observation and experiment on the hypothesis of their equal objectivity, and entered on a career of dazzling conquest, without troubling itself to invent any philosophical justification for a method so prolific of discoveries as to silence all criticism or cavil by the brilliancy of its achievements, philosophy had already entered upon a path which led indeed to the construction of numerous subjective systems of unsurpassed ability, yet to none that could endure. The history of philosophy has been for three centuries only a succession of gaily-coloured pictures, each more startlingly beautiful than the last, yet each doomed to disappear at the next turn of the kaleidoscope. While science can proudly point to a vast store of verified and established truths, which it is a liberal education to have learned and the merest lunacy to impugn, philosophy has achieved nothing that is permanently established. The cause of this vast difference in result is a radical difference in method. (Objectivism, albeit solely empirical, has created the glory of science; subjectivism, albeit elaborately and ostentatiously reasoned,) has created the shame of philosophy. And philosophy can never redeem itself from this shame of utter barrenness until it repudiates subjectivism with Nominalism, its cause.

The epoch of Scholasticism is regarded by some as closed by the death of Gabriel Biel, the "last Scholastic," in 1495, when Nominalism had acquired almost undisputed sway.

Now the essential method of Scholasticism had been, as Tennemann well expresses it, to "draw all knowledge from conceptions". So long as Realism flourished, and universals, as entities, were held to possess substantial objective existence, the analysis of concepts, independently of experience or verification, was held to yield real knowledge of their objective correlates—a mistake impossible to the New Realism or Relationism. But when Nominalism had destroyed the objectivity of universals, it had also destroyed the possibility of deriving objective knowledge from concepts. A dilemma thus arose: either objective knowledge is unattainable, or it must be attained otherwise than by the mere analysis of concepts as such. But how?

In this manner was developed a new and momentous problem, that of the Origin of Knowledge, which now displaced the old and still unsolved problem of the Nature of Universals—not at all fortuitously, but logically and inevitably as a direct result of the triumph of Nominalism. Nominalism had answered the old question after its own manner by resolving universals into merely subjective notions; and this answer, false as it was, was accepted as satisfactory. But the acceptance of it involved some awkward consequences. If objective knowledge cannot be derived from concepts, whence can it be derived? Or is there no such thing as objective knowledge?

Science met these questions by boldly adopting the principle of Objective Verification—a principle depending absolutely for its philosophical justification on the theory of Relationism, but adopted by Bacon and the inductionists in general as a purely empirical method, in utter indifference to such justification. From that time forward, scientific men have (quietly assumed the objectivity of relations) and steadily pursued the path of discovery in total disregard of the disputes of metaphysicians—not, however, without a serious loss to science itself, in the growth and spread of the false belief that science can legitimately deal only with physical investigations, and that the scientific method has no applicability in the "higher sciences".

But philosophy met the same questions by dividing into two hostile camps. The sufficiency of the Nominalistic answer to the question of universals—that they are exclusively of subjective origin—was taken for granted by both parties; genera, species, relations of all kinds, were unanimously conceded to possess no objective validity whatever. Logically, (this is the total surrender of all objective knowledge; and in the long run modern philosophy has come to accept this result,) as shown by the almost entire unanimity of modern philosophers in the opinion that things-in-themselves, or noumena, are utterly incognoscible. But it is impossible to maintain this opinion in logical consistency, and on this point not a single logically consistent philosopher can be pointed out; if he can be found, he will prove to be an inexorably rigorous Solipsist, not afraid to deny the existence of all minds save his own, no less than that of the material world. It would be refreshing to meet with a subjectivist possessed of the courage of his opinion; but he would be the terror of all his brother-subjectivists, perhaps a candidate for premature interment.

The division that now arose and separated modern philosophy into two great contending parties, did not concern the question whether knowledge originated in the object or in the subject,—for both parties agreed in the Nominalistic answer to this question,—but whether, in the subject mind itself, it originated in the senses or in the intellect. That was the great new question started at the recognised dawn of modern philosophy by Descartes and Locke; and both parties to the controversy, both the *à priori* and the *à posteriori* schools, were equally switched off upon the false track of Nominalism that conducts to Egoism or to nothing.

Descartes' theory of "innate ideas" encountered a vigorous rival in Locke's theory of experience as limited to the data of "sensation and reflection"; and thus the two armies took position for the long warfare that is resultless still. There is not the slightest occasion, for the purposes of this paper, to follow the course of this dispute, or to repeat the argumentation and counter-argumentation by which it has been maintained. The point of view here taken is that both these famous schools have logically immured themselves in the dungeon of subjectivism, and are utterly powerless to release themselves; that the one is just as incompetent as the other to explain the "origin of knowledge" about which they have been contending so long; and that, like Venus and Mars suspended in Vulcan's cage to provoke the "inextinguishable laughter" of the Odyssean gods, they do but enact a farce at which philosophy hangs her head. Travelling round the same circle of subjectivism in opposite directions, these two schools are fated to re-unite on the farther rim in one identical point—the stand-point of Absolute Egoistic Idealism. That is the only possible terminus of a subjectivism that, beginning with (the definition of knowledge as only the mind's recognition of its own states) dares to obey the logic of its own fundamental principle; and what is the philosophy worth that contradicts itself? No sequent thinker who begins with the Ego as sole starting-point will fail to end with the Ego as sole terminus, unless he stoops to unworthy tricks or evasions; and that is the suicide of philosophy.

The triumph of Nominalism did indeed force upon thought a new problem in the question of the "origin of knowledge"; but great is the delusion of the two schools which imagine the solution of that question to lie with one of themselves.

The *à priori* school started with Descartes' *Cogito ergo sum;* that is, with an original positing of the Ego as an *individual thinking being*. The *à posteriori* school started with Locke's "sensation"; that is, with an original positing of the Ego as an *individual feeling being*. That is essentially the only difference —the difference between beginning with individual thought or individual feeling as the prior element of individual consciousness,—both beginnings being equally and incontrovertibly egoistic. But this is a trivial difference indeed, compared with the abysmal difference between both these egoistic schools, on the one hand, and modern science, on the other; for here the issue is a broad, deep, fundamental one—namely, whether the real "origin of knowledge" is in the Ego or in the Non-Ego, or in both. (Knowledge itself, in the conception of both these Nominalistic schools, is confined to the series of changes that go on in consciousness;) and all their mutual discussions are mere child's-play, compared with the discussions that await philosophy the moment she comes abreast of the time.

Science is to-day challenging emphatically the very foundation of both *à priori* and *à posteriori* philosophies; and the challenge is none the less menacing or deep-toned, because it has been hitherto uttered in deed rather than word. She denies, not by a theory as yet, but by the erection of a vast and towering edifice of verified objective knowledge, that genera and species are devoid of objective reality, or that general terms are destitute of objective correlates; she denies that Nominalism has rightly solved the problem of universals, when that solution would in an instant, if conceded, sweep away all that she has won from Nature by the sweat of her brow. Her very existence is the abundant vindication of Relationism, as the stable and solid foundation of real knowledge of an objective universe. As the case now stands, philosophy has two great schools, equally founded on a reasoned subjectivism which *denies the possibility of knowing*, in any degree, an objectively existent cosmos as it really is; while science rests immovably on the fact that she *actually knows* such a cosmos, and proves *by verification* the reality of that knowledge which philosophy loudly and emphatically denies. Science must be all a huge illusion, if philosophy is right; philosophy is a sick man's dream, if science is right. One or the other must speedily effect a total change of base; and it is safe to predict that the change will not be made by science.

Three answers are given, therefore, to the question as to the Origin of Knowledge; two by Nominalism, with its two schools of modern philosophy, and one by Relationism, interpreting the silent method of science. They are substantially as follows:—

(1) The *à priori* school teaches that knowledge has two ultimate origins, the experience of the senses and the constitution of the intellect—the senses contributing its *à posteriori* "matter" and the intellect contributing its *à priori* "form"; that the intellect is the source of certain universal and ante-experiential principles of knowledge which cannot be in any manner derived from the senses; that these principles or "forms" are themselves an object of pure *à priori* cognition, independently of experience; that experience consists solely of sense-phenomena, and sense-phenomena give no knowledge of their merely hypothetical noumenal causes, *i.e.*, of "things-in-themselves". In other words, things (if they exist—which is at least dubious) conform themselves to cognition; the subject knows only its own subjective modifications, arranged in a certain order according to *à priori* laws of knowledge which are only subjectively valid. This is Nominalistic Subjectivism of the *à priori* type.

(2) The *à posteriori* school teaches that knowledge has only one ultimate origin, the experience of the senses; that the intellect is indeed the source of certain universal constitutive principles of knowledge, but that these were originally derived from the senses, having been slowly organised and consolidated, by the law of the "association of ideas," into hereditarily transmissible "forms" of experience; that there is no such thing as "pure *à priori* cognition," independent of experience; that experience consists solely of sense-phenomena, that the intellect itself has been slowly evolved out of it, and that sense-phenomena give no knowledge of their merely hypo-

thetical noumenal causes. In other words, things-in-themselves (if they exist—which is equally dubious by this theory) conform themselves to cognition (the subject knows only its own subjective modifications) arranged in a certain order according to *à posteriori* laws of knowledge, which are only subjectively valid. This is Nominalistic Subjectivism of the *à posteriori* type.

Thus both of these dominant schools thoroughly agree in planting themselves upon the foundation of Moderate Nominalism or Conceptualism; they agree that universals, the genera and species by which alone sense-phenomena are reducible to intelligible order, are merely subjective concepts without objective correlates. They agree that things-in-themselves are unknown and unknowable, and that the subject knows its own conscious states alone. By both schools, consequently, the principle of Relationism is either unknown or ignored; relation itself is by both reduced to a merely subjective category, valid only as the subjective order imposed on subjective sense-phenomena, and utterly meaningless as applied to noumena; and noumena—intelligible objective realities, as presented by the various sciences—are totally incognoscible. But when the vitally pertinent question is put: "*Why* should the series of sense-phenomena, or sensations, or consciousnesses in general, be what it is? *Why* should the senses and understanding conspire to give a coherent appearance of objective knowledge, when no objective knowledge is possible?" neither school has any reply to make. The only reply consistent with their common premises would be Fichte's reply, that the apparent objects of knowledge are given by the subject to itself, according to some inscrutable law working subtly beneath consciousness itself. This reply has at least the merit of consistency with the ground-principles of subjectivism, and does not flinch from landing philosophy in Solipsism undisguised. But few subjectivists possess sufficient hardihood to make this consistent reply; they prefer to "have their cake and eat it too".

(3) The theory of Scientific Philosophy (by which is meant simply the philosophy that founds itself theoretically upon the practical basis of the scientific method) teaches that (knowledge is a dynamic correlation of object and subject) and has two ultimate origins, the cosmos and the mind; that these origins unite, inseparably yet distinguishably, in experience, *i.e.*, the perpetual action of the cosmos on the mind *plus* the perpetual reaction of the mind on the cosmos and on itself as affected by it; that experience, thus understood, is the one proximate origin of knowledge; that experience has both an objective and a sub-

jective side, and that these two sides are mutually dependent and equally necessary; that the objective side of experience depends on the real existence of a known universe, and its subjective side on the real existence of a knowing mind; that experience includes all mutual interaction of these, whether sensitive or cognitive, and is utterly inexplicable even as subjective sensation, unless its sensitive and cognitive elements are equally recognised; that this extended conception of experience destroys the distinction of noumena and phenomena, as merely verbal and not real; that "things-in-themselves" are partly known and partly unknown; that, just so far as things are known in their relations, they are known both phenomenally and noumenally, and that the possibility of experimentally verifying at any time their discovered relations is the practical proof of a known noumenal cosmos, meeting every demand of scientific certitude and furnishing the true criterion and definition of objective knowledge. In other words, science proceeds upon a principle diametrically opposite to that of Nominalism, already explained under the name of Relationism. It assumes that cognition conforms itself to things, not things to cognition, —that being determines thought, not thought being,—that the subject knows not only its own subjective modifications but also the objective things and relations which these modifications reveal. Kant did but "assume" the counter-principle; and if he considered his assumption as at last "demonstrated" by his system as a whole, science equally considers its assumption as demonstrated by the actual existence of its verified and established truths as a body of objective knowledge.

These three answers to the question as to the origin of knowledge show how vast is the divergence between modern philosophy and modern science. Philosophy has never yet entirely shaken off the blighting influence of Scholasticism, even while fancying itself wholly emancipated from it; for Nominalism, no less than the old Realism, was the legitimate offspring of Scholasticism. It was only one of the two great answers, both one-sided and both wrong, which Scholasticism gave to the question of universals. Philosophy is still Scholastic to-day; it has never yet modernised itself in any true sense, and it never will do so until it sits modestly at the feet of science, imbues itself thoroughly with the spirit of the scientific method, and applies the principle of Relationism to the reconstitution of the moral sciences and the total reorganisation of human knowledge. This, though a vast revolution for philosophy herself, will be simply giving in her adhesion to the revolution which science made long ago, and has rendered irreversible. But it will also be putting herself at the head of that revolution, and conducting it to conquests in regions of the highest truth of which science herself has never yet dreamed.

IV.

Aristotle taught, with truth, that the proper object of science is the universal rather than the particular or individual. Although it was his doctrine that individuals are First Essences, while species are Second Essences, and genera Third Essences, real only in a lower sense than the former, nevertheless it was also his doctrine that the universal inheres in each individual substance and constitutes its conceptual or intelligible essence (ἡ κατὰ τὸν λόγον οὐσία). The universal and the individual were inseparable, and must therefore be known together: yet the universal, being the essence of the individual, was itself the only proper and real object of scientific cognition.

Translating the Moderate Realism of Aristotle into the more accurate language of Relationism, and not forgetting to correct its capital error of making the universal inhere in each individual as an individual *(in re)* rather than in all the individuals as a group *(inter res)*, the meaning of his doctrine is that science is concerned with the general relations of things rather than with the things themselves—with general laws rather than with the peculiarities or accidents of individual objects.

Modern science proceeds uniformly according to this incontestable principle. Says Prof. Jevons:—

"There is no such process as that of inferring from particulars to particulars. A careful analysis of the conditions under which such an inference appears to be made shows that the process is really a general one, and what is inferred of a particular case might be inferred of all similar cases. All reasoning is essentially general, and all science implies generalisation. In the very birth-time of philosophy this was held to be so: 'Nulla scientia est de individuis, sed de solis universalibus,' was the doctrine of Plato, delivered by Porphyry. And Aristotle held a like opinion; Οὐδεμία δὲ ἐπιστητόν. 'No art treats of particular cases, for particulars are infinite τέχνη σκοπεῖ τὸ καθ' ἕκαστον . . . τὸ δὲ καθ' ἕκαστον ἄπειρον καὶ οὐκ and cannot be known.' No one who holds the doctrine that reasoning may be from particulars to particulars can be supposed to have the most rudimentary notion of what constitutes reasoning and science."

It is, in truth, impossible to study even a particular case without generalising; all knowledge consists in the seizure of the relations of things, and every name of a relation is of necessity a general term. Prof. Jevons correctly quotes both Plato and Aristotle as concurring in this fundamental principle, since both of them occupied the stand-point of objectivism; and Prof. Jevons himself, as a scientific man, can occupy no other, although, as a thinker, more or less infected with the subjectivism of modern philosophy, he has not succeeded in occupying it always or with entire consistency.

Now subjectivism reduces all science to the knowledge of *one individual*, the Ego,—which, as just shown, is no science at all. If its fundamental definition of knowledge means anything, or is faithfully adhered to, subjectivism teaches that the intelligent subject has no intelligence save of itself—has no warrant for believing in the existence of anything save itself—knows nothing but the inexplicable order of its own sensations and thoughts. It reduces all existence to an unrelated One, while of an unrelated One no science is possible. In a word, subjectivism, if logical, annihilates science at a blow.

There is no logical escape from this inference, drawn directly from the subjectivist definition of knowledge. Subjectivism cannot concede the knowledge of any existence except that of the subject itself; it cannot concede any knowledge of the subject, except that of its seriated conscious states; it cannot concede any knowledge of these conscious states as a series, but only as single and unrelated; and it thus lands ultimately in the scepticism of Hume. For to generalise a series of thoughts as *thought*, or a series of sensations as *sensation*, is to use a general term, which, *ex hypothesi*, corresponds to no existent correlative in an objective sense; the general terms, thought, sensation, consciousness, on the principle of Nominalism, denote nothing real in the thoughts, sensations or consciousnesses which are generalised, but express only an act of the subject as generalising. Apply the very same principle to the knowledge of the subject itself which subjectivism applies to the knowledge of the outer world,—refuse that objective validity to general terms as applied to the world of consciousness which is refused to general terms as applied to the world outside of consciousness,—and it is shown irresistibly that subjectivism does not permit "knowledge" even of the subject's own "conscious states". "Consciousness" is a general term; "state" is a general term; every such term denotes a relation among certain related objects; and if this relation must be separated from the related objects when they are *outside of the subject*, why must it not be separated from the related objects when they are *within*? Subjectivism necessarily destroys itself by its own definition of knowledge; it cannot exist an instant except by denying the very principle it asserts; it escapes self-annihilation only on the hard and humiliating condition that it shall perpetually contradict itself. The sword with which it slays science pierces its own heart.

Nothing is more astonishing than the utter indifference of

subjectivists to their own innumerable self-contradictions on these vital points—self-contradictions all the more amusing in view of their insistance that objectivism shall be rigorously and consistently reasoned. Let a few instances be here noticed.

Berkeley's idealism (a direct product of the Nominalistic revolution) is usually praised to the skies as unerringly logical and self-consistent. Yet the same reasoning which leads him to deny the existence of a material world ought to lead him to deny the existence of other human minds—of which there is no proof except sight, hearing, and touch of the material bodies by which these minds manifest themselves. Berkeley's great paralogism on this point is pointed out even by his own editor, Dr. Krauth (p. 400), as follows:—

"Berkeley is a realistic idealist; holding that the realistic inference is invalid as regards matter, but conceding it as regards mind. He holds to real substantial spirits, God and man. Hence, too, his monism is only generic. He holds to a monism of genus,—to spirit alone; but he concedes a dualism of species,—infinite Spirit, the cause of ideas, and finite spirits, the recipients of them. But this his strength is also his weakness. Every moral advantage of his Idealism over its successors is secured at the expense of its development and of its logical consistency."

Mr. Shadworth H. Hodgson, in his *Time and Space* (Introduction, p. 5), says:—

"By the term consciousness, in this Essay, is always meant consciousness as existing in an individual conscious being; and proofs drawn from such a consciousness can have no validity for other conscious beings, unless they themselves recognise their truth as descriptions applicable to the procedure and phenomena of their own consciousness. Doctrines, if true, will ultimately be recognised as such by all individuals whose consciousness is formed on the same type, that is, by all human beings."

Here is luminously presented the cardinal and universal contradiction in all non-solipsistic form of subjectivism: (1) The assumption that the Ego knows only the changes of its own consciousness; and (2) the assumption that the Ego knows other Egos to exist that are "formed on the same type". One of these assumptions necessarily destroys the other.

There are countless similar self-contradictions scattered all through the writings of subjectivists, some amusing by their *naïveté*, some ingenious in their subtlety, some amazing by their evident unconsciousness, but all sufficiently humiliating and mortifying to those who would fain see philosophy comport herself with the dignity of science rather than with the agility of a circus-clown. One further illustration will suffice.

Prof. Clifford, in his *Lectures and Essays* (ii. 71), takes the ground of the most uncompromising subjectivism at the outset, and then coolly proceeds to break loose from it in the most violently illogical style, yet apparently without the least suspicion of the exhibition he thereby makes of himself as a philosopher :—

"The objective order, *quâ* order, is treated by physical science, which investigates the uniform relations of *objects* in time and space. Here the word *object* (or *phenomenon*) is taken merely to mean a group of my feelings, which persists as a group in a certain manner ; for I am at present considering only the objective order of my feelings. The object, then, is a set of changes in my consciousness, and not anything out of it. . . The inferences of physical science are all inferences of my real or possible feelings ; inferences of something actually or potentially in my consciousness, not of anything outside of it."

Bald and unblushing as is the egoism of this passage, it is entirely clear; and it is quite possible to build up on this basis an idealistic Solipsism which shall at least tolerably cohere with itself. But Prof. Clifford immediately proceeds to crucify his own subjectivism in this manner :—

"However remote the inference of physical science, the thing inferred is always a part of me, a possible set of changes in my consciousness bound up in the objective order with other known changes. But the inferred existence of your feelings, of objective groupings among them similar to those among my feelings, and of a subjective order in many respects analogous to my own,—these inferred existences are in the very act of inference *thrown out* of my consciousness, recognised as outside of it, as not being a part of me. I propose, accordingly, to call these inferred existences *ejects*, things thrown out of my consciousness, to distinguish them from *objects*, things presented in my consciousness, phenomena. . . . How this inference is justified, how consciousness can testify to the existence of anything outside of itself, I do not pretend to say : I need not untie a knot which the world has cut for me long ago. It may very well be that I am myself the only existence, but it is simply ridiculous to suppose that any body else is. The position of absolute idealism may, therefore, be left out of count, although each individual may be unable to justify his dissent from it."

This airy distinction of "object" and "eject" does not in the least disguise the cardinal contradiction into which Prof. Clifford, in common with all subjectivists who shrink back from Solipsism, falls. Ejects, as he proceeds to define them, are simply "other men's minds"; but other men's minds are only known through their bodies, and their bodies are "objects" like trees or stones ; while trees and stones are just as truly "ejects" from consciousness as are other men's minds. In a word, ejects are objects, and objects are ejects ; there is absolutely no distinction between them, on Prof. Clifford's own showing; objects and ejects must be both objective or both subjective. Yet Prof. Clifford arbitrarily (it would almost seem wilfully) objectifies ejects and subjectifies objects ! He flatly refuses to "untie a knot" which contains the whole point in dispute, and which the "world" has "cut" just as effectively for objects as for ejects; he coolly begs the whole question, and repudiates the Solipsism from which his own principles permit no rational escape.

These illustrations of the self-contradiction of subjectivism are *typical*, not *sporadic*; they show how deep-rooted is the disease under which modern philosophy is suffering. Whenever (if ever) subjectivism shall dare to be rigorously logical, it will be the *reductio ad absurdum* of Nominalism, and compel philosophy to adopt Relationism and the scientific method in general. All science is of the universal; all sequent subjectivism abolishes the universal, and leaves only the individual, a solitary, unrelated, incomprehensible Ego. It avails nothing to create a phantom-science of the universal in a world of sensations alone; true philosophy, no less than true science, demands an explanation of that series of sensations which subjectivism can accept only as an unintelligible fact. Diogenes commanded a certain respect so long as he actually lived in his tub; but if, having fastened to his forehead a placard, "I am Diogenes, and I live in this tub," he had then tied the tub to his back, lived in a house, slept in a bed, and behaved like ordinary mortals, he would have been pelted with a storm of pitiless gibes from the keen-witted Athenians. And when philosophy, having tied the tub of subjectivism to its back, lives and lectures in a world of "ejects," and expounds to them a science of the objective relations they bear to each other and to an intelligible cosmos, human nature must have radically changed if philosophy fares any better.

It all comes to this; either the truth of subjectivism or the truth of science is a pure illusion. The possibility of the one is the impossibility of the other.

The conclusion just stated finds abundant corroboration in contemporaneous thought. Subjectivism in philosophy has created a new type of scepticism in science. Urged as it were by a consciousness that it can only maintain its own truth by discrediting the truth of science, philosophy does not hesitate to undertake the task. Hence it has formulated a law of philosophical scepticism under the name of the "relativity of knowledge," founded upon a truism, but distorted into a falsity. Unable to shake the conviction of the reality of a known objective universe, and therefore unable to take the field in its only logical form of Solipsism, subjectivism nevertheless covertly saps the truth of science in a manner which hides its own fatal inconsistency. It declares that all knowledge is merely relative to human faculties, and it adroitly pushes this principle as if relativity were unreality. A quotation from Mr. Frederic Harrison's essay on "The Subjective Synthesis" will well illustrate the mode of its attack:—

"The truly relative conception of knowledge should make us habitually feel that our physical science, our laws and discoveries in Nature, are all imaginative creations—poems, in fact—which strictly correspond within the limited range of phenomena we have before us, but which we never can know to be the real modes of any external being. We have really no ground whatever for believing that these our theories are the ultimate and real scheme on which an external world (if there be one) works, nor that the external world objectively possesses that organised order which we call science. For all that we know to the contrary, man is the creator of the order and harmony of the universe, for he has imagined it."

This subjectivistic scepticism, be it remembered, has its root in the Nominalism which universally prevails in philosophic circles, and which has profoundly affected those scientific men who, being more than mere specialists, have felt their influence; and it shows exactly where science must seek aid from a renovated philosophy, if it is to escape suffocation by the firedamp of scepticism engendered by its own operations. "If every genus is only a mere word," says a writer in the *Encyclopædia Britannica*, "it follows that individuals are the only realities, and that the senses are at bottom the only sources of knowledge. And not only so, but on this theory no absolute affirmation respecting truth is possible, for such an affirmation involves of necessity a general idea, which *ex hypothesi* is destitute of real validity. Hence we have scepticism at the next remove." Mr. Harrison is an illustration of the literal accuracy of this statement. But the case is not bettered if the genus is "only a mere" *concept*, instead of "only a mere word"; for Extreme Nominalism and Conceptualism (the latter of which this writer accepts) are equally sceptical in their implications, since they equally disown the objectivity of relations. Only the theory of Relationism fully meets the case.

The doctrine of the "relativity of knowledge," under cover of which subjectivism makes its attack on the objective truth of science, undoubtedly rests on a truism: namely, that knowledge is itself a relation between the knowing and the known, and that nothing can be known except as it is known by the knowing faculties. This, surely, is a very innocent proposition. It simply means that man cannot know everything; it does not at all mean that he does not know what he knows. That human knowledge of the cosmos is incomplete, partial, inadequate, could be controverted only by a consistent subjectivist, to whom the cosmos is simply the sum of his own sensations or consciousness, which, again, exist only as they are known. But the doctrine of the relativity of knowledge, properly construed, has a real validity and profound significance to the objectivist, since it states the fact on which the total activity of science rests—the fact that human knowledge is small, and can be increased. There is nothing whatever in this doctrine to discourage science or impugn the solid character of its acquisitions. From the very nature of the case, nothing but relative knowledge is possible. Increase the number and scope of man's cognitive faculties till his science becomes omniscience: his knowledge will still be relative, being the relation of knowing and known, and that unconditionally. In fact, "non-relative knowledge" is a contradiction *in adjecto*. As Prof. Ferrier puts it in his *Remains*: "To know a thing *per se*, or *sine me*, is as impossible and contradictory as it is to know two straight lines enclosing space; because mind by its very law and nature must know the thing *cum alio*, *i.e.*, along with itself knowing it". The doctrine of the relativity of knowledge, therefore, is a truism so far as it asserts the co-essentiality of subject and object to the relation of knowledge; it is a falsity and absurdity so far as it asserts the non-knowableness of the object by the subject in that very relation of knowledge. And the blade of subjectivism is shivered in its very grasp by the adamantine shield of science.

Nevertheless it remains true that the progress of science is retarded and embarrassed by the prevalence of a philosophy which secretly undermines its results, controverts its fundamental postulate of the knowableness of the objective universe, and dooms it to an imperfect comprehension of the principles which alone justify its practical procedure. A philosophical vindication of those principles which should establish the scientific method, so resplendently successful in its empirical employment, upon an impregnable rational theory, could not fail in ten thousand ways to promote the advancement of knowledge, and dissipate that cloud which hangs over the deeper thought of our own age—the cloud of an intellectual consciousness at war with itself. Every attempt in this direction should be greeted with a hearty welcome.

Let us review the situation, and state the problem distinctly which Philosophy has now to solve.

Subjectivism in philosophy takes its stand, consciously or unconsciously, on Nominalism. Its fundamental principle is the law, accepted by both the Transcendental and Associational schools, that things conform themselves to cognition, not cognition to things. The necessary corollary of this law is the *separability of phenomena and noumena*, phenomena having their existence solely as modifications of the individual consciousness, and noumena either having no existence at all or else existing solely as the unknown and unknowable causes of phenomena. Of these two alternatives, the former alone is logically consistent with the premisses of subjectivism; for, since "cause" is a universal term to which Nominalism denies all objective validity or significance, it is a term patently inapplicable to anything beyond the sphere of subjective consciousness. Hence the final outcome of all thoroughgoing subjectivism is absolute egoistic Idealism or Solipsism—a mere cosmos of objectively causeless dreams.

Objectivism in science takes its stand, consciously or unconsciously, on Relationism. Its fundamental principle is the law of Objective Verification,—that cognition must conform itself to things, not things to cognition. The necessary corollary of this law is the *inseparability of noumena and phenomena*, phenomena being the "appearances" of noumena, and noumena being that which "appears" and is partially understood in phenomena; and they have their inseparable existence, not only in the mind, but also in the cosmos which the mind cognises. The only utility in retaining the distinction at all is to mark the distinction between complete and incomplete knowledge—noumena being taken to denote things-in-themselves as they *exist* in all the complexity of their objective attributes and relations, and phenomena being taken to denote these same things-in-themselves so far only as they are *known* in their objective attributes and relations. The final outcome of scientific objectivism is a constantly growing knowledge of the real cosmos as it is, in which the human mind has its proper place and activity in entire harmony with cosmical laws.

This is the unequivocal issue between the two modes of viewing the universe which are confusedly and half-consciously struggling for supremacy in the modern mind. Philosophy is prevailingly subjective, but not wholly so; there are occasional symptoms of secret restiveness among philosophers under the iron yoke of Nominalism, such as the appeal of the Scotch School to "Common Sense," the "Natural Realism" of Hamilton, the "Reasoned Realism" of G. H. Lewes, the "Transfigured Realism" of Mr. Herbert Spencer, the "Inferential Realism" of Rev. J. E. Walter and many others, the unmistakably objective tendencies of the historian Ueberweg—who explicitly declares that "the objective reality of relations can be affirmed with at least as much reason as it can be disputed" (*Hist. Phil.* I, 374), and that "the demonstrative reasoning by which we go beyond the results of isolated experience, and arrive at a knowledge of the necessary, is not effected independently of all experience through subjective forms of incomprehensible origin, but only by the logical combination of experiences according to the inductive and deductive methods on the basis of the order immanent in things themselves" (*Ibid.* II., 162),—as well as of others that might be named in this connexion. But no one, even among these uneasy insurgents against the established tyranny of Nominalism, seems to comprehend exactly what the tyranny or who the tyrant is; no one of them seems to have traced back the origin of his oppression to the half-forgotten decision, arrived at centuries ago by the now despised Schoolmen, as to the nature of universals; and no one seems to comprehend precisely what will free him from fetters that are invisible, yet strong as steel. Hence every one of them continually falls into concessions which rivet the fetters more closely about his limbs. The hostility secretly existing and working between the subjectivist and objectivist methods, even in one and the same mind, is one of the curious and striking features of contemporaneous thought, and will not fail to arrest the attention of the future historians of philosophy. Yet this antagonism between science and philosophy is really unnatural and injurious in the last degree, for they are the natural complements and allies of each other. Science needs the intellectual orderliness and systematic unity which philosophy alone can create; philosophy needs the verified basis and thoroughly objective spirit of science. Hence our age presents no problem more profound in its nature, or more wide-reaching in its bearings upon the intellectual interests of mankind, than this:—

How to identify science and philosophy, by making the foundation, method, and system of science philosophic, and the foundation, method, and system of philosophy scientific.

The theory of knowledge which is predominant in both the Transcendental and Associational schools of modern philosophy has been clearly set forth in the preceding pages, traced to its source in the wrong answer given by mediæval Nominalism to the questions of universals, and shown to impart even to so-called modern philosophy a thoroughly Scholastic character. The theory of knowledge which underlies the practical procedure of modern science has also been clearly set forth, although only so far as its fundamental principle is concerned, under the name of Scientific Realism or Relationism,—the full development of which will involve the creation of a new and comprehensive philosophical system. The irreconcilable antagonism of these two theories, the disastrous consequences of it both to philosophy and science, and the necessity of a profound revolution in the method of philosophy in order to bring it into harmony with the now thoroughly established scientific method, have likewise been shown, together with the precise nature of the problem which philosophy has now to solve, in order to modernise itself in a true sense.

All that is here possible is simply to state the problem and the general principle on which alone it can be solved; a full solution of it is the great desideratum of science and philosophy alike. For a full solution of it will permanently heal the breach which now disastrously divides them, and for the first time render possible the harmonious coöperation and concentration of all the powers of the human mind for the discovery, establishment and application of cosmical truth. What has been here done is to show that this greatest of modern problems is only, under a new form, that ancient and never satisfactorily answered question of Universals which, for hundreds of years, absorbed the brightest intellects of Europe,—to submit to the bright intellects of our own time, together with the old half-answers to that problem historically known as the theories of Nominalism and Realism, a third, new and full answer in the theory of Relationism,—and to inquire whether this theory will not suffice to bring about the greatly needed identification of Science and Philosophy.

FRANCIS ELLINGWOOD ABBOT.

Printed by Libri Plureos GmbH in Hamburg,
Germany